THE **OCTOBERBABY** BIBLE STUDY
STUDENT EDITION

IS BEAUTIFUL

Written by Pam Gibbs
Based on the film by Jon and Andrew Erwin
Screenplay by Theresa Preston and Jon Erwin

LifeWay Press®
Nashville, TN

ISBN: 9781415873106
Item Number: P00548879
Dewey Decimal Classification Number: 179
Subject Heading: ABORTION \ SELF-ACCEPTANCE \ PRO-LIFE MOVEMENT

Printed in the United States of America

Student Ministry Publishing
LifeWay Church Resources
One LifeWay Plaza
Nashville, TN 37234-0174

We believe that the Bible has God for its author; salvation for its end;
and truth, without any mixture of error, for its matter and that all Scripture
is totally true and trustworthy. The 2000 statement of *The Baptist Faith
and Message* is our doctrinal guideline.

Table of Contents

ABOUT *OCTOBER BABY*

OCTOBER BABY is the coming-of-age story of Hannah, a beautiful 19-year-old college freshman. In spite of her energetic (if somewhat naïve) personality, Hannah has always felt like an outsider. Something is missing. She has always carried a deep seeded sense that she has no right to exist.

When she discovers she was adopted it comes as a shock, but Hannah's world is rocked even more when she learns why she was never told before—because she was the survivor of a failed abortion. Desperate for answers, she embarks on a road trip with some friends (including her oldest and closest friend, Jason) to find her biological mother. Ultimately, Hannah discovers that true freedom can be found in the words "I forgive you" as she discovers who she is and receives the peace to live the life she has always dreamed.

This uplifting and beautiful film may change the way you look at the world, your loved ones … and life.

You may want to visit *www.octoberbabymovie.net* and *www.lifeway.com/octoberbaby* for updates and more information.

STUDY THEMES
The Power of Secrets
The Search for Identity
The Path of Forgiveness
The Joy of Restoration

ABOUT THE AUTHORS

THE ERWIN BROTHERS

OCTOBER BABY director team Jon and Andrew Erwin have been working in the entertainment industry for many years. Both began their careers as sports cameramen for ESPN.

In 2005 the pair ventured into directing commercials and music videos. They found their greatest success in the world of music, directing music videos and producing concerts and television programs for platinum artists and groups like Amy Grant, Michael W. Smith, Third Day, and Casting Crowns. The Erwin brothers have received 10 nominations and back-to-back wins for Music Video of The Year at the GMA Dove Awards.

Recently, the brothers completed on location in the Galapagos, a feature-length documentary titled *The Mysterious Islands*.

Andy and Jon are based in Birmingham, Alabama, where they own their own production company. Filmed in various locations across Alabama, *OCTOBER BABY* is their first feature film.

PAM GIBBS worked alongside the Erwin brothers to develop this Bible study. Pam serves as the girls' ministry specialist at LifeWay Christian Resources. She has contributed to many student ministry resources through the years, including *James: Faith Under Pressure*.

LETTER TO READERS

What is your definition of a nightmare? Showing up to class and realizing you didn't study for a big test? Being chased by something or someone you can't see? Maybe it's the fear of a family member or best friend? Maybe it's being unable to mend a relationship.

But what if your worst nightmare wasn't something you could predict, but something that came out of nowhere and shook your very foundation?

That's the story of Hannah. She has faced challenges that many of us could never understand—surgeries, health concerns, and deep feelings of despair. In OCTOBER BABY, Hannah discovers the root of her pain: She is an abortion survivor. On top of that, she was adopted and never knew it. Everything she knew suddenly gets thrown into question.

OCTOBER BABY is Hannah's journey toward discovering not only who she really is, but also who God really made her to be. The movie is a powerful picture of a young woman who learns that life is beautiful, each and every part of it.

OCTOBER BABY is as much about the beauty of life as the sanctity of life. As Hannah searches for her biological mother, she finds herself and a renewed faith in God. As a result, you will probably relate to the characters, even if the specific details don't match your own story.

Think of this Bible study resource as an opportunity to jump into a swimming pool. The characters and clips are the diving board, but the Word of God is the water. When you jump in, you'll land in the middle of Scripture that will challenge you to evaluate how your life and your story align with the truth of God's Word. Our prayer is that you will discover new truth about God and be challenged to openly live that truth.

Life is beautiful. It's composed of stories that make it real, sometimes raw, but always rich with opportunity to live out the redemptive story of Jesus.

SESSION 1
The Power of Secrets

OPEN UP
Secrets. Everyone has them.

Some secrets are silly. For example, I carry a secret affection for the music of Barry Manilow. (Go ahead and Google him on your phone so you'll know who he is). I know—it's cheesy and odd and, um, very nerdy and outdated. Now that you know this particular secret, you can understand why I don't tell anyone.

Of course, this secret is not particularly damaging. In reality, it's sort of silly. But that's not unusual. Most people have some things they'd rather keep to themselves: secretly wanting to meet New Kids on the Block, being a closet collector of unicorns, or the fact that you still sleep with your toy dinosaur your dad gave you when you were three.

What silly secrets do you keep?

On the other hand, some secrets are not so silly. Some secrets are not so insignificant and irrelevant. In fact, some secrets are incredibly painful, powerful, and damaging.

Want to know how to tell if a secret is not-so silly? Fill in the blank: *If you knew _____ about me, you wouldn't like/love/accept me.* The things that you would use to fill that blank are the things that hit close to home for you. Those are the dangerous secrets in your life.

The abuse you endured. The abortion you had. The taunting of a bully you face. The addiction to pornography you cannot control. The questions you battle about your sexual identity. The suicidal fantasies that dominate your thoughts. Those dark secrets can take a lot of different forms, but they hurt all the same.

Kept to yourself, these secrets can multiply in their intensity. The longer they stay hidden, the deeper they grow. They take root and, in time, take over your life.

Watch It
View Clip 1, "The Secret Revealed" (3:04), from the small-group DVD.
Summary:
In this scene, a 19-year-old young woman, named Hannah Lawson, discovers that her parents have been keeping a secret from her—a secret about how her life began—or almost didn't begin. It is a secret that will shake her understanding of who she is.

Dive In
What's true in this movie is also revealed to us in Scripture. Remarkably, the Old Testament provides a case study for what happens when a secret sin is just that—kept secret. It shows what one man was willing to do to cover up his sin, as well as the consequences he and others endured because of his powerful secret.

Meet David
David is one of the most well-known characters in the Bible. He killed lions, bears, and giants. He was a musician and poet. He was even known as a "man after God's own heart."

Unfortunately, he was an adulterer and murderer.

If you haven't read the story, that's OK. Here it is, from 2 Samuel 11:1-15:

¹ In the spring when kings march out to war, David sent Joab with his officers and all Israel. They destroyed the Ammonites and besieged Rabbah, but David remained in Jerusalem.
² One evening David got up from his bed and strolled around on the roof of the palace. From the roof he saw a woman bathing—a very beautiful woman. ³ So David sent someone to inquire about her, and he reported, "This is Bathsheba, daughter of Eliam and wife of Uriah the Hittite."

⁴ David sent messengers to get her, and when she came to him, he slept with her. Now she had just been purifying herself from her uncleanness. Afterwards, she returned home. ⁵ The woman conceived and sent word to inform David: "I am pregnant."

⁶ David sent orders to Joab: "Send me Uriah the Hittite." So Joab sent Uriah to David. ⁷ When Uriah came to him, David asked how Joab and the troops were doing and how the war was going. ⁸ Then he said to Uriah, "Go down to your house and wash your feet." So Uriah left the palace, and a gift from the king followed him. ⁹ But Uriah slept at the door of the palace with all his master's servants; he did not go down to his house.

¹⁰ When it was reported to David, "Uriah didn't go home," David questioned Uriah, "Haven't you just come from a journey? Why didn't you go home?"

¹¹ Uriah answered David, "The ark, Israel, and Judah are dwelling in tents, and my master Joab and his soldiers are camping in the open field. How can I enter my house to eat and drink and sleep with my wife? As surely as you live and by your life, I will not do this!"

¹² "Stay here today also," David said to Uriah, "and tomorrow I will send you back." So Uriah stayed in Jerusalem that day and the next.

¹³ Then David invited Uriah to eat and drink with him, and David got him drunk. He went out in the evening to lie down on his cot with his master's servants, but he did not go home.

¹⁴ The next morning David wrote a letter to Joab and sent it with Uriah. ¹⁵ In the letter he wrote:

Put Uriah at the front of the fiercest fighting, then withdraw from him so that he is struck down and dies.

In David's day, the roofs weren't slanted—they were flat.

The story goes like this (in my loose translation): David can't sleep so he goes for a stroll on the roof of his palace, where he had an unobstructed view of his domain and his people. One of those people was Bathsheba. He sees her. Likes her. Asks about her. And finds out she's married. But this doesn't stop David. He summons her to the palace, has sex with her, and sends her home. Nice.

Bathsheba really had no idea that David was on his roof. The Bible tells us kings marched off to war with their armies that time of year. She had no way of knowing that he was there. Nothing negative is said about Bathsheba.

David's Secret Sin

If David had turned around and walked back into the palace, the whole messy, sordid, painful mess could have been avoided. But he didn't, and so we learn something about secrets:

Secrets often stem from a sinful action.

David took what didn't belong to him. He misused his power for his own pleasure. Later on, Bathsheba shared some news that rocked David's selfish world: she was pregnant.

Oops. I don't think that was in David's plans.

And so began his slavery to secrets.

If Bathsheba had decided to ignore the king's summons, David could have had her killed.

Here's how secrets might develop in your life. Sometimes, you sin; sometimes, another person sins and you bear the shame. Either way, sin puts you in a position where you want to hide the truth—and that creates the need for a dangerous secret.

GUYS' PERSPECTIVE

You lust over a girl—so you develop elaborate sexual fantasies.

Your dad left you—so you take drugs to feel better.

Your coach threatened to bench you—so you take steroids for an edge.

GIRLS' PERSPECTIVE

A girl likes your ex-boyfriend—so you start a rumor about her.

A guy rapes you on a date—so you don't tell anyone.

Your mom ignores you—so you cling to anyone who will be nice to you.

What secret in your life has stemmed from sin—whether that sin be yours or someone else's?

The Deception Deepens

If David had confessed his secret, he would have endured the consequences of his actions, which, according to the law, might have been death. But he could have done so with a clear conscience and a cleansed heart. Unfortunately, David didn't learn from his first secret. And so the secrets piled up.

David liked what he saw. There's no sin and no secret in that. Seeing a person as attractive isn't wrong in itself. But what you do about that attraction makes all the difference.

David brought Uriah home from the battle in hopes that he would be intimate with his wife. Then, it would appear that he was the father of her child. But that didn't work. So David tried again, only this time he got Uriah drunk. But his hopes that alcohol would weaken Uriah's standards didn't pan out either. Uriah's upright character put the sinful David in a tough spot. And so we learn another truth about secrets:

Secrets pile on top of one another.

Twice, David tried to hide his infidelity by enticing Uriah to be with his wife. Eventually, when none of that worked (ironically because Uriah was a man of incredible character), the king ordered Joab, his general, to make sure Uriah died in battle. Then he made his soldiers lie to cover up how Uriah had died. Then after the "time of mourning ended" David brought Bathsheba home to be his wife (2 Sam. 11:16-27).

Obviously, David was a real jerk. He definitely wasn't acting like a man after God's heart.

David's secrets piled on top of one another, but so do yours. Here's how it might look:

GUYS' PERSPECTIVE

You've been gambling online. To keep playing, you secretly steal money from your dad's wallet. When that money runs out, you bribe your sister into giving you cash, threatening to tell your parents about her low grades if she tells anyone.

You've become the target of a bully's rage. To hide your embarrassment over not being "strong enough" to fight, you always come up with an excuse for why you were late to class or why you have strange bruises on your face. When you get detention for being late, you tell your parents you're at a friend's house instead of telling them the truth.

GIRLS' PERSPECTIVE

You've been dating a guy that your parents don't like. To spend time with him, you sneak behind their backs, saying that you'll be at the mall with your friends when you really intend to meet your crush there and drive somewhere else. While in his car, you're hit broadside. You have to secretly cover up your bruises with make-up and lie about the scrapes.

Everybody thinks you've got it all together, but you feel empty inside. You feel like you don't have any friends, your parents don't understand you, school stinks, and you think you'd be better off dead. You secretly get into your mom's prescription pills and steal a few at a time. When you have enough, you can take them later. To make sure no one suspects, you keep acting like everything is OK.

How have you seen secret sins pile up?

Secret's Control

When David found out Bathsheba was pregnant, his life spun out of control with the all-consuming need to cover up his secret. He was determined that no one would find the flaw in his character, and it changed the course of his life. He learned a tough lesson:

Secrets can control you.

David should have been thinking about his kingly duties—like managing the war Uriah was so committed to fighting. He should have put his energy into other areas. Instead, this one secret controlled him. He was driven to cover up his actions, whatever the cost. In the end, the man who had once written about the Author of life stooped so low as to take a life to keep his actions secret. And that secret controlled him.

How have you seen secrets control an area of your life? How did you find freedom from that slavery to secrets? In what areas do you still need freedom?

GUYS' PERSPECTIVE

The longer you take steroids, the more you begin to rely on them. Eventually, you can't control the rage that comes out of nowhere.

Your addiction to porn leads you to longer and longer spans online. You start to act out what you're seeing on the screen.

Your dad's abuse dominates the way you relate to others. In response, you're not about to let anyone know how much he hurts you.

GIRLS' PERSPECTIVE

Your addiction to porn means you're lying to friends, hiding stuff from your parents, and fantasizing about guys in your class.

Life is chaotic—grades, family, friends, the team. The only thing you can control is food. You are driven to eat less in an effort to find physical perfection. Nothing else matters.

Every other girl you know seems to be attracted to guys, but you really aren't. You secretly start chatting online to another girl about how you feel about girls. You become obsessed with your new online friend who understands you. You decide to meet at the mall and see where the relationship might go.

The Weight of Secrets

I cannot imagine bearing the secrets that David carried—knowing that he slept with another man's wife, tried to cover it up twice, killed the man, and then covered up the murder. What that weight must have done to his energy and his spirit. Scripture actually tells us how he felt in Psalm 32:3-4.

> ³ *When I kept silent, my bones became brittle*
> *from my groaning all day long.*
> ⁴ *For day and night Your hand was heavy on me;*
> *my strength was drained*
> *as in the summer's heat.*

David learned a big lesson:

Secrets wear you out.

You understand how he felt, don't you? You probably haven't committed murder, but you know what it's like to carry a secret—a big secret—and how the weight of it can kill you from the inside out. That addiction. That abuse. The shoplifting. The struggles with body image. The temptations to click on that certain Web site. The weight of what's really going on is almost more than you can bear.

But you're scared to let the secret find the light of day. What will people think of me? What will _____ do if she/he finds out? What would my parents do? What if I get rejected? Or yelled at? Left alone?

I understand. It's like a devastating war inside your mind that leaves your stomach and your emotions in knots. But don't despair. There is one more truth in this story.

Don't Despair—There Is Hope

The end of 2 Samuel 11 sounds pretty bleak: "…the LORD considered what David had done to be evil" (v. 27). But that's not the end of the story. In the end, David learned one more truth:

Secrets lose their power when shared.

Psalm 32:5-7 (which David wrote, by the way) goes on to say:
> ⁵ *Then I acknowledged my sin to You*
> *and did not conceal my iniquity.*
> *I said,*
> *"I will confess my transgressions to the LORD,"*
> *and You took away the guilt of my sin.*
> ⁶ *Therefore let everyone who is faithful pray to You*
> *at a time that You may be found.*
> *When great floodwaters come,*
> *they will not reach him.*
> ⁷ *You are my hiding place;*
> *You protect me from trouble.*
> *You surround me with joyful shouts of deliverance.*

Of course, God loved David too much to let him go on as if nothing had happened. That's why He sent a prophet named Nathan to confront the king and to challenge him to confess his sin (2 Sam. 12:1-15). When David finally came clean before God, things changed. God took away the guilt. The flood of shame and disgrace receded. He wasn't consumed and defined by his secret any more.

Only when these secrets are laid bare can they lose their power to control you. Otherwise, you remain captive. You're a prisoner of the very lies you thought would give you freedom!

I was talking to a friend one day about something that I had been keeping to myself, something I had not shared. I told her that I felt like a balloon that could burst at any moment. Maybe that's exactly how you feel, too. The intensity and the weight of the secret is bearing down on you, and you're about ready to burst.

Here's the good news: when you share your secret in a safe place, the pressure eases—like letting air out of a balloon. Whether you did something wrong or something wrong was done to you, there is great relief in giving voice to what has happened. Talking to someone won't make everything go away. But it's a good first step toward healing.

Live It

Keeping secrets leaves you lonely. You feel isolated. No one else could possibly understand. You think no one else would ever do what you've done. But the truth is this: *Everybody* struggles. *Everybody* has been wounded in some way.

We either share our secrets, or, eventually, our secrets ooze out somehow and tell their own stories. To find healing and freedom, we need to be the ones who expose the secrets. It might get harder before it gets better, but sharing leads to a better, more authentic life.

What secrets are you keeping?

How would you describe the intensity of your secret?

How has this secret changed your life?

Who would be a safe person, someone with whom you could share the burden of that secret?

When you think of sharing your secret, what objections pop into your head? Based on what you learned from David's example, why is it important to overcome those objections?

Remember, your secrets really aren't secrets with God. He knows and understands. And He loves you, right where you are.

SESSION 2
The Search for Identity

OPEN UP
Who am I?

Every teenager asks that question. And every teenager spends these critical years trying to find the answer.

Everything about you is changing—your appearance, your friendships, your emotions, and your ability to process information. And those changes spark questions about who you really are. It's not about what your parents want, what your friends assume, or what your teachers expect. It's about the person you want to become.

Under the best of circumstances, answering "Who am I?" is hard. But when you harbor a secret (one of those secrets that need to be told), answering the question of who you are becomes even more difficult, almost impossible. Why?

Because sometimes your secret defines you.

I am a victim. I am an addict. I am an anorexic. I am a bully. I am forgotten. I am abused. I am a failure. I hate myself.

The good news is that you are more than the sum of your secrets. Defining yourself by your secret is like saying, "I'm an arm." You have an arm, but you are a person. You have a secret, but you are much more than that.

Watch It
View Clip 2, "I Don't Even Know Me" (4:34) from the small-group DVD.
Summary:
In this scene, Hannah has recently learned that not only is she adopted, but she's also the survivor of a failed abortion. Trying to process her

thoughts, she sits on a dock where she'd played as a child. Jason, her best friend (and potential romantic interest), joins her at the dock. He can sense something's wrong, and he wants to hear what's on her mind.

Dive In

Hannah's identity was radically shaken by the news surrounding her birth and her birth mother. In the movie she says, "My whole life is a lie... I don't even know me." Have you ever felt that way? Like you don't even know you? That feeling probably comes up when your identity is questioned in some way. To understand how your identity is questioned, though, you first need to understand what you base your identity on.

And for guys and girls, it's different.

GIRLS' PERSPECTIVE

Girls define themselves by relationships. Most problems in a girl's life will stem around a relationship—a friend, a boyfriend, a parent, a mean girl, a teacher, and so forth. Who you are in terms of those around you matters a lot. You value and strive to maintain relationships. You are constantly aware of how your behavior affects others (and their perceptions of you). Your world looks like an intricate web of relationships. One writer has even compared the way girls approach relationships to a plate of spaghetti noodles.

Get a group of girls together and what do you do? You talk. You relate.

GUYS' PERSPECTIVE

In contrast to girls, guys define themselves by their accomplishments, by their ability to do something. What can you dominate? A game? A sport? A car? For you, it's all about being competent and strong and capable and able. It's about conquering the world around you.

That's why the top video games on the market for teen boys involve a gun, a fast car, or a sport. It's all about what you can do. Get a bunch of guys together and what do you do? Compete at something, from burping contests to video games.

So, what's so important about the way you define yourself? The answer is really pretty simple:

Identity formed apart from God is flawed and erratic.

Meet Saul . . . I Mean, Paul

One prominent New Testament character learned this lesson, and he shared his story with us. Here's what he said, from Philippians 3:3-14.

3 For we are the circumcision, the ones who serve by the Spirit of God, boast in Christ Jesus, and do not put confidence in the flesh— 4 although I once had confidence in the flesh. If anyone else thinks he has grounds for confidence in the flesh, I have more: 5 circumcised the eighth day; of the nation of Israel, of the tribe of Benjamin, a Hebrew born of Hebrews; regarding the law, a Pharisee; 6 regarding zeal, persecuting the church; regarding the righteousness that is in the law, blameless.

7 But everything that was a gain to me, I have considered to be a loss because of Christ. 8 More than that, I also consider everything to be a loss in view of the surpassing value of knowing Christ Jesus my Lord. Because of Him I have suffered the loss of all things and consider them filth, so that I may gain Christ 9 and be found in Him, not having a righteousness of my own from the law, but one that is through faith in Christ —the righteousness from God based on faith. 10 My goal is to know Him and the power of His resurrection and the fellowship of His sufferings, being conformed to His death, 11 assuming that I will somehow reach the resurrection from among the dead.

12 Not that I have already reached the goal or am already fully mature, but I make every effort to take hold of it because I also have been taken hold of by Christ Jesus. 13 Brothers, I do not consider myself to have taken hold of it. But one thing I do: forgetting what is behind and reaching forward to what is ahead, 14 I pursue as my goal the prize promised by God's heavenly call in Christ Jesus.

Before . . .

The life of Paul is like watching a house being renovated. At the beginning, all you see is a dilapidated shack that threatens to collapse with the next strong breeze. In the end, though, the guts have been ripped out, and everything has been completely changed.

Or think about a car restoration. What amounts to a heap of junk in the beginning undergoes a real transformation as the master craftsmen do their magic. The end result is a machine that makes guys drool.

Before his amazing conversion (check out Acts 9), Paul defined himself by his stellar record as the perfect, God-fearing Jew. Here are some of the descriptions that he was once proud of, along with a "translation":

- circumcised on the eighth day *(Translation: my parents were devout Jews who made sure I followed the Law from birth.)*

A medical procedure performed eight days after his birth, circumcision was a rite to outwardly mark a boy as a Jew. It was a sign of his covenant relationship with God. The law said that uncircumcised men had no place in Jewish faith or practice.

- of the nation of Israel *(Translation: I am a descendant of the patriarch Jacob, the founder of Israel, so my lineage goes back further than yours.)*
- of the tribe of Benjamin *(Translation: unlike other tribes that turned away at some point, my tribe was always faithful.)*

Jacob (Israel) had 12 sons, who became the 12 tribes of Israel.

- a Hebrew of Hebrews *(Translation: Unlike some Jews who were Greek, Paul was a Hebrew Jew born to Hebrew parents. He had a perfect ancestral line of Judaism.)*
- a Pharisee *(Translation: I am among an elite group of Jews who followed our religion to the strictest end.)*

Pharisees were an influential group of Jewish men who believed that religious ritual and separation from "sinners" was the only way to please God and to prepare for His coming.

- Zealous persecutor of the church *(Translation: I believed so much in my religion that I did everything I could to stamp out Christianity, including killing people. See Acts 9 for proof!)*

- Flawless *(Translation: I'd done everything the law could promise. I had not failed any Jewish standard.)*

If you'd have asked Paul the question, *Who are you?*, his answer would have been, "I am a Jew." His identity was wrapped up in doing everything right by Jewish standards.

Answer this question: Who are you?

...And After

Paul was content with his life as a devout Jew until he discovered that there was something more, something greater and better that would truly define him. Here's how he put it:

But Christ has shown me that what I once thought was valuable is worthless. Nothing is as wonderful as knowing Christ Jesus my Lord. I have given up everything else and count it all as garbage. All I want is Christ and to know that I belong to him. I could not make myself acceptable to God by obeying the Law of Moses. God accepted me simply because of my faith in Christ." (Phil. 3:7-9, CEV)

Paul acknowledged that everything he once thought was true was actually a lie. The things he considered valuable were like garbage. Trying to do everything right wasn't what made him right, and being "perfect" as a Jew wasn't all life had to offer.

When have you wondered if there was more to your life than doing everything right?

Having your identity stripped away can be scary. What happens when you're no longer the smartest in the class or no longer relying on drugs to get you through the day? When you're no longer a tough athlete? When your dad leaves? When you aren't the most popular?

Does that scare you? Paul wasn't scared to leave his old life because he had found something greater and higher. He discovered something permanent in which he could ground his identity: his relationship with Christ.

You are not the sum of your mistakes.

You may have lived your entire life thinking your identity relied on something you did, like being a scholar or an athlete or most popular or most ignored. You may have thought that you were defined by something done to you—sexual abuse, physical abuse, rape, conditional approval, being accused of something you didn't do, or bullying. At some point, you need to understand that identity formed apart from God is flawed and erratic. It's warped, and it's not real.

Jeremiah 2:13 says, "For My people . . . have abandoned Me, the fountain of living water, and dug cisterns for themselves, cracked cisterns that cannot hold water." Often, we choose to forsake our identity as children of God—the only identity that's enough to get us through the struggles of life. Instead, we try to create our own "cisterns," our own wells. But our cisterns are useless and beyond repair. They will never satisfy us. Only God can do that.

We are flawed, sinful, and inconsistent people. Our actions and behavior are always changing, for better or for worse. The good news is that, just like Paul, you can find your true identity in Christ.

Only in Him (outside of your own accomplishments, achievements, and relationships) can you find a reliable source of identity. He provides an identity that doesn't rely on someone else's opinions, an identity that cannot be lost or gained based on your success or failure, an identity that isn't defined by something in your past.

Restoration Has Begun

It would be completely understandable if Paul had chosen to define himself by his actions as a Jew. And it would make perfect sense to us if he had defined himself by his mistakes. (He was a murderer, after all.)

But that wasn't Paul's attitude at all. Instead of rooting his purpose and meaning in his old way of life, he defined himself by something rooted in eternity—what Jesus had done for him on the cross. He had learned a life-altering truth:

Because of Christ, our true identity has been restored.

Around the time Paul wrote Philippians, he also wrote a letter to the church at Colossae. In that letter, he gave his readers some great news:

"For the entire fullness of God's nature dwells bodily in Christ, and you have been filled by Him, who is the head over every ruler and authority." (Col. 2:9-10)

Life outside of Christ is empty. In contrast, life with Christ is full. It may not be easy all the time, but it certainly is not empty. When you come to Christ in faith and turn your life over to Him, the very mission of your life is transformed. You have been restored into a right relationship with God that changes everything about you. Your life gains hope and meaning.

- Living for yourself lacks genuine purpose and meaning. Living for Christ is an adventure.

- Living in the past is meaningless. Living to fulfill God's plan for your present and future is exhilarating.

- Living to protect yourself leaves you feeling tired and empty. Living in a community of faith is fulfilling.

- Living in your mistakes leads to a cycle of pain. Living as a forgiven child of God brings healing and freedom.

"No one can make you feel inferior without your consent." —Eleanor Roosevelt

Live It

Just like Paul, you must choose where your identity will be grounded. Take a few minutes and think through what's shaping the way you see yourself. What defines you? What do you use to answer the question raised earlier in the session: *Who am I?*

- **By a relationship:** I am _____'s _____

- **By what you do:** I am a(n) _____

- **By what was done to you:** _____ wounded me by _____

- **By what you did to someone else:** I wounded _____ by _____

Now work through these questions, asking God to teach you more about who you are in His eyes . . .

How has this identity been difficult to maintain?

What do you think it would be like to be free of that label?

Who are some people you have labeled? How can you help them discover who they are in Christ?

God understands the human need for identity and meaning. That's why Scripture contains so many verses that remind us who we are as a follower of Christ. You can find a few examples below. Meditate on them this week and memorize at least one that holds a special significance to your life.

- **You are God's child (John 1:12)**
- **You have been chosen by God (Eph. 1:3-8)**
- **You have been redeemed and forgiven (Col. 1:13-14)**
- **You are complete in Christ (Col. 2:9-10)**
- **You are free from condemnation (Rom. 8:31)**
- **You cannot be separated from God's love (Rom. 8:35)**
- **You have been bought with a price (1 Cor. 6:19-20)**

In the movie, Hannah goes around the country, but she had to come home to remember who she really was. She was loved—by God and her family. You are a lot like her. Apart from Christ, you'll meet disappointment wherever you go. Only when you come back home will you remember who—and whose—you are. (Read Luke 15:11-32 for the story of someone else who looked for purpose, only to find it on his own doorstep.)

You are God's. And that is always enough.

But you may realize that you can't find your identity in Christ because you really don't know Him as your Lord and Savior. If that's where you find yourself, you can start that relationship today—right now. Simply say a prayer like this:

Dear God, I know I'm a sinner and have tried to find happiness apart from You. I believe Jesus died for my sin and only through faith in His death and resurrection can I be forgiven and freed to be the person You want me to be. I now turn from my sin and ask Jesus to come into my life as my Savior and Lord. From this day forward, I choose to follow Jesus.

If you prayed that prayer, share it with your small group leader. He or she can help you take your first steps of obedience as you begin your journey with Christ.

SESSION 3
The Path of Forgiveness

OPEN UP
"I forgive you."

Someone once said that these are some of the most powerful words ever strung together in a single sentence. But it also raises some interesting questions that require some wrestling on our part. For example,

- But what does forgiveness mean, really?
- Does forgiving a bully mean you want to be friends now?
- Does forgiving the child molester mean you have to forget what he or she did to you?
- Does forgiving yourself mean you can do whatever you want?
- Does forgiving a person once mean you'll never have to forgive him or her again for the same offense?
- Does forgiving your parents for divorcing mean you're happy they split up?

With all the myths, quotes, and sayings about forgiveness (like, "love means never having to say you're sorry"…seriously???), it's hard to figure out what it really means to forgive. The good news is that Scripture gives us plenty of examples.

Watch It
View Clip 3, "You Have the Power to Forgive" (6:51) from the small group DVD.
Summary:
In this scene, Hannah seeks answers to her questions in a place that was once a refuge for her adoptive mom. While in the cathedral, she meets a priest who helps her discover the importance and the power of forgiveness. She learns that only in forgiveness can she be free.

Dive In

Hannah's world was upside-down. She was angry with her parents for withholding the truth about her adoption. She felt betrayed, confused, angry, and wounded because her biological mother tried to abort her when she was born—and then denied her once they finally met face-to-face. She felt guilty for surviving when her twin brother died soon after their birth. To top it all off, Hannah was angry at herself for all the turmoil she was feeling in her life.

While you may not be dealing with the same issues as Hannah, you can probably relate to her feelings. You know the sting of betrayal. You've been wounded when someone has lied to you. You've been angry at yourself and others—maybe even an intense anger that you fear will leap out of your chest at any minute. You've hurt others and others have hurt you—certainly in small ways and, possibly, in life-changing ways.

No matter what the offense or how deep (or fresh) the wound, there is one underlying truth:

Forgiveness offers the only real way to find freedom from the hurt.

GIRLS' PERSPECTIVE

Typically girls offer forgiveness through their words. Why? Because girls are relational. They talk. A lot. So it would make sense that they would use words to express themselves, including those times when they need to express remorse. They're quick to say whatever needs to be said to restore a relationship.

How do you typically try to apologize when you've hurt someone?

GUYS' PERSPECTIVE

Guys don't typically say they are sorry. They don't typically ask someone for forgiveness. Why? Because in their minds, apologizing to someone is the same as admitting a mistake. And that's really difficult for guys to do. Remember, guys often base their worth on their successes, so failure can be crushing to a guy. It's easy for pride to get in the way.

How do you typically express the fact that you've done something wrong? Why do you choose that way to say you're sorry?

Sibling Rivalry Gone Wrong

One of the coolest stories in the Old Testament centers around two brothers who didn't always get along (does that make you feel better about your family?). Jacob and Esau were twins, but that's where their similarities end.

They were polar opposites. Esau, the hairy hunter, was favored by his dad. Meanwhile, Jacob, the quiet, stay-at-home type, was a little bit of a mama's boy.

These two battled it out for decades until a huge blow out sent Jacob running for his life because Esau threatened to kill him. And the two didn't see each other for more than 20 years. The relationship between the two of them changed only after God spoke to Jacob in a dream. (If you want the whole story, read Genesis 25–32.)

When they finally did meet up again, the reunion of the two brothers was the stuff of movies. Jacob was sure Esau was ready to kill him over their old grudge. But he wanted to make one more effort at reconciliation. Genesis 33:1-11 tells us how it went down . . .

¹ Now Jacob looked up and saw Esau coming toward him with 400 men. So he divided the children among Leah, Rachel, and the two female slaves. ² He put the female slaves and their children first, Leah and her sons next, and Rachel and Joseph last. ³ He himself went on ahead and bowed to the ground seven times until he approached his brother.

⁴ But Esau ran to meet him, hugged him, threw his arms around him, and kissed him. Then they wept. ⁵ When Esau looked up and saw the women and children, he asked, "Who are these with you?"

He answered, "The children God has graciously given your servant."
⁶ Then the female slaves and their children approached him and bowed down. ⁷ Leah and her children also approached and bowed down, and then Joseph and Rachel approached and bowed down.

⁸ So Esau said, "What do you mean by this whole procession I met?"

"To find favor with you, my lord," he answered.

⁹ "I have enough, my brother," Esau replied. "Keep what you have."

¹⁰ But Jacob said, "No, please! If I have found favor with you, take this gift from my hand. For indeed, I have seen your face, and it is like seeing God's face, since you have accepted me. ¹¹ Please take my present that was brought to you, because God has been gracious to me and I have everything I need." So Jacob urged him until he accepted.

Did you notice that Jacob never actually apologized for his past actions? Jacob used his actions to express his apology instead of relying on his words—true to the character of most guys.

Truths We Can Discover

Esau and Jacob's reunion is a story of forgiveness that reveals some truths for us to ponder:

• **It's never too late to forgive.** Jacob and Esau hadn't seen each other for more than 20 years; but at God's prompting, the two came together to give and receive forgiveness. And from what we can pick up from the Scriptures, the gestures of grace were genuine.

What's the longest time you've held a grudge against someone? How long has someone been at odds with you? You may think that fixing what went wrong is an impossible task after all that time. This story is a reminder that forgiveness doesn't have an expiration date.

• **Forgiveness doesn't mean everything goes back to normal.** If you read a little further in the story, you'll discover this little gem of truth.

Genesis 33:16-17 tells us that "Esau started on his way back to Seir, but Jacob went on to Succoth." Did you catch that? They didn't go back to the farm to live together as one big, happy family. They reconciled, but they also parted ways.

Seir and Succoth were a good distance apart in camel-riding standards, so they probably didn't spend the holidays together. In fact, the Bible indicates that Jacob and Esau probably never saw each other again until they buried their father years later (Gen. 35:29).

You may think that if you forgive someone, everything has to return to normal. You may think you're supposed to act as if nothing happened or that you're supposed to be good friends or happy family members. But that's just not the case. Forgiving someone doesn't automatically mean that you want to pursue a relationship with him or her, especially if that person abused you severely. And that's perfectly OK.

Forgiveness is the final form of love.—Reinhold Niebuhr[1]

On the flip side, you may have hurt someone deeply. While you may receive forgiveness, the consequences of your actions don't go away. If you bullied someone and got arrested, you'll still face punishment. If you had an abortion, you can be forgiven, but you still bear the emotional and physical consequences. Those don't go away automatically.

Think of someone you need to forgive. What was your relationship like before he or she hurt you? What would you like your relationship with that person to look like after you've forgiven him or her?

You have the right to set healthy boundaries for your relationships. Because of that, forgiving someone does not mean that you have to subject yourself to further negative treatment.

1. http://www.brainyquote.com/quotes/topics/topic_forgiveness.html#ixzz1gRGluczb

• **Forgiveness is a balm that heals not only the offender, but also the victim.** Even the medical community recognizes the negative effects of holding a grudge.

> • You can get so wrapped up in the past that you cannot enjoy the present.
> • You can become depressed or anxious.
> • You may feel like your life lacks meaning.
> • You bring anger and bitterness into every relationship.
> • Your relationship with God suffers because He is in the business of reconciliation (not grudges).
> • You lose connection with others because you're afraid that something negative might happen again.[2]

When you harbor unforgiveness, it's like drinking poison and expecting the other person to die. You think you're getting back at the person, but you're really only hurting yourself.

What negative consequences have you experienced because of harbored resentment, anger, and unforgiveness?

In our story, Jacob and Esau both changed. The night before Jacob met Esau for the first time in decades, he had a life-altering (and name-changing) encounter with God (Gen. 32:24-32). The story is a bit mysterious, but we do know that Jacob came away from that encounter as a humbled man, willing to bow to the ground to meet his brother.

Seeing the change in Esau is a little more difficult. There's no record of a God-encounter, but we know Esau was a changed man. Why? Because "Esau ran to meet him [Jacob], hugged him, threw his arms around him, and kissed him" (Gen. 33:4). These are not the actions of a man still committed to killing his brother (Gen. 27:41). The grudge was gone; the anger had subsided, and forgiveness, however miniscule and imperfect, had taken root in Esau's heart.

---

2. http://www.mayoclinic.com/health/forgiveness/MH00131

Think of a time when you harbored a grudge against someone. What was your motive for choosing *not* to forgive? What was the end result for both you and the other person?

One More Biblical Truth

There's one more important truth to learn about forgiveness, but it's not found in the story of Esau and Jacob. It's actually found in the Scripture that was quoted in this week's video clip:

Therefore, God's chosen ones, holy and loved, put on heartfelt compassion, kindness, humility, gentleness, and patience, accepting one another and forgiving one another if anyone has a complaint against another. Just as the Lord has forgiven you, so you must also forgive.
—Colossians 3:12-13

Here's the truth: **Because you have been forgiven, you have the power to forgive.** Jesus died on the cross for you and me to experience the forgiveness and grace of God. We were bound up in our own chains of sin and death, but His death and resurrection gave us the key to unlock those chains. Now, because we have been set free (John 8:31-32), we have the capacity and ability to set others free with our forgiveness. The grace of God is a gift to be shared, not hoarded.

Think about this: Paul wrote the letter to the Colossians while he was in jail. Life as a follower of Christ wasn't easy. But Paul had been transformed by the grace and mercy of God (check out Acts 9), and that transformation changed him forever.

Forgiving others is never easy, and I doubt it was a picnic for Paul. In fact, forgiving someone else just might be the hardest thing you've ever done. But it is possible because God forgave you. While you can never do it on your own, you can find the strength to forgive others through Him.

The practice of forgiveness is our most important contribution to the healing of the world. —Marianne Williamson[3]

If you're having a really difficult time letting go of some hurt from your past, you might need to ask yourself whether or not you've really accepted God's grace and love. If you're still living like you're trying to earn your way back onto God's good side, you've never really let the tender mercies of God wash over you.

And you can't give to others something you've never received.

How does it feel to know that God has forgiven you? What makes you hesitant to offer that same mercy and grace to someone else?

OK, But How?

Right now, you might be thinking, "OK, I get it. I need to forgive. But how do I do it? Do I click my heels three times and say a magic word?"

There is no five-step plan to achieve forgiveness. Forgiveness is both a choice and a process that takes time and space for healing. However, here are a few tips that will help you in that journey:

1. Let go of your anger. Anger is a natural response to being hurt. But after a while, anger can cause more harm than good. Making the choice to stop being angry doesn't mean the other person gets off the hook. It just means that don't want anger to define your life.

2. Turn your desire to be the judge over to God. It's not your job to make the other person pay for their sins. That's God's job, as painful as it is to admit. Again, you can hold a grudge if you choose, but you're the one that suffers in the end. Understand that God is righteous, and He will make things right in the end.

3. http://www.brainyquote.com/quotes/topics/topic_forgiveness3.html#ixzz1gRH32gQ3

3. Focus on the present, not the past. If you continually talk about what happened in the past, you will never be able to live in the present or look forward to the future. You'll be paralyzed, which is not a healthy way to live your life.

4. Express yourself. If it won't make the situation worse, talk to the person who has offended you. If you think open discussion will cause a greater rift (or if you don't want to continue the relationship), find another way to express yourself. Write a letter and tear it up (or burn it). Paint. Draw. Build something. Just do something to put a voice to your feelings.

5. Continue to forgive. If the wound was deep, you'll probably have to forgive more than once. When a memory surfaces, don't allow yourself to get worked up again and again. Instead, say to yourself, "I choose to forgive. I already forgave." Ask God to give you the grace to forgive again. And again. And again. After all, that's how He treats us.

No one ever gets to the end of life and says, "I wish I had been more angry. I wish I would have harbored more resentment." Most of us, when looking back, will wish we had forgiven more.

"Her many sins have been forgiven; that's why she loved much. But the one who is forgiven little, loves little."—Luke 7:47

What Forgiveness Looks Like
After Hannah talks with the priest about forgiveness in "October Baby," she chooses to express forgiveness to her birth mother who tried to have her aborted—and later rejected her as an adult. Hannah writes "I forgive you" on a piece of paper and places it (along with the I.D. bracelet from the hospital when Hannah was born) on her birth mother's desk.

The scene depicts what it is like to offer—and receive—forgiveness.

Sometimes, forgiving yourself is harder than forgiving others.

The Last Piece of the Puzzle

"October Baby" deals with forgiving others, but it's also about forgiving yourself. Any woman confronted with the child she tried to abort will have to decide whether or not she will accept forgiveness from God, others, and especially from herself.

Your story may be very different than the biological mother in the movie. Perhaps you are guilty of other things—lust, anorexia, bullying, drug or alcohol abuse, sexual assault, verbal abuse or something else. Regardless of the source of your guilt, the question in front of you is the same: *Can you forgive yourself?*

Just like forgiving others, forgiving yourself isn't just a matter of following a simple plan for instant success. However, there are some truths you can embrace to help you along the journey toward healing:

- Recognize that you are not the sum of your mistakes. You may have failed miserably, but you are not a failure. Remember session 2? Your identity is not based on your performance, but on the fact that God sees value in you and loves you. Deeply.
- Confess your sins to God. Accept His forgiveness.
- Make amends where possible. Ask for forgiveness from others. Ask others to hold you accountable for your actions. Change your habits to prevent similar offenses from happening again.
- Don't wallow in guilt or shame. Self-punishment won't get you anywhere—except on everyone else's nerves.
- Give to others. Volunteer at the hospital. Donate money to an abuse shelter. Work at a soup kitchen. Not only will it help you feel better about yourself, but it will also remind you that we're all gloriously flawed and in need of grace.

Live It

All of us have been wounded. Every one of us has been both the offender and the target of someone's spite, anger, or fears. God wants to heal you—no matter what wound you bear. The following exercise can help you walk through the process of forgiving someone.

- Prayerfully ask God to reveal any anger, bitterness, spite, or resentment you're holding against others. Give the Holy Spirit all the time He needs to speak to you about what is buried or hidden in your heart.
- Write down what God reveals to you, even if it seems trivial.
- Place a chair facing you. Imagine that the first person on your list is sitting in the chair. Speak your hurt aloud to him or her. If this makes you nervous, write a letter instead. Do not hold back any emotion as you speak or write.
- Choose to say, "I forgive you." You may not feel particularly merciful or compassionate. That's OK. Your feelings will catch up with your actions later.
- Thank God for being the Source of forgiveness. Ask Him to fill you with the grace and compassion necessary to truly forgive.
- Repeat the steps above for every person God reveals to you as you pray. If time will not allow, choose another time in the near future to repeat this process.
- Continue to forgive. Remember, forgiveness is both an event and a process.

One Word to the Wounded

Some wounds are too deep and too heavy to carry alone. If you are the victim (or the victimizer) of abuse—whether physical violence, emotional trauma, or sexual addiction or violence—you will benefit from professional counseling. Talk with your parents about your struggles and ask them to help you find a counselor who can help you.

A Christian therapist trained in helping people process hurts can help you unload and process the memories and events that you've been storing up in your mind and heart for far too long. Finding professional help isn't a sign of weakness. It's a sign that you are determined to be whole again.

SESSION 4
The Joy of Restoration

OPEN UP

Flip through the channels on your television and you'll probably come across some show about building and restoring something. Trick out your car. Fix your basement in 48 hours. Rebuild a house in a week. Follow this "simple" routine to sculpt six-pack abs. Complete eight steps to create the perfect bathroom.

What makes me stop at one of those shows is the big "reveal." That's when you get to see the "before" and "after" pictures that show the dramatic difference between the old and the new. *Wow*, I think to myself, *I could do that!* Seeing the end result motivates me.

God is the Master Rebuilder. His specialty isn't anything physical, like cars, muscles, or bathrooms. He specializes in taking the broken pieces of our lives, restoring them, and showing them off as an "after" picture—a picture of grace in motion.

Watch It

View Clip 4, "Thank You for Wanting Me" (3:07) from the small group DVD.

Summary:

This clip, at the end of the movie, shows several scenes in which restoration takes place. An abortive woman finds healing and forgiveness from not only the child she tried to abort, but also from her husband. A nurse who had worked for an abortion clinic finds a new life as a labor and delivery nurse. And a father and daughter reconnect. In the end, we celebrate life, as beautifully flawed and imperfect as it is this side of heaven.

Dive In

The Bible is full of adjectives and titles to describe God: El Elyon, Adoni, Counselor, Author and Finisher of our faith, El Shaddai, Abba, Almighty, and many others. Although not expressly stated in the Bible, you can add another title to that list: *Restorer of broken lives.*

GIRLS' PERSPECTIVE

The Bible is filled with stories of women God used to do amazing things despite their checkered pasts. Rahab, the prostitute of Jericho. The woman at the well. Mary Magdalene. Tamar and Ruth. Even Martha, the busy-body. Most of them even had a "skeleton" in their closet. But they also serve as a reminder that, in God's hands, even the most wrecked of lives can be restored to a beauty that only His healing can bring.

GUYS' PERSPECTIVE

It seems like God specializes in taking broken men, healing them, and using them for His purposes. They are all role models that guys look up to: David (an adulterer and murderer), Moses (a murderer), Paul (an enemy of the church), Peter (an arrogant hothead), Nicodemus (a legalist with a lot of questions). None of them were perfect. In fact, they each had serious sins included in their list of accomplishments. But all of them still experienced the thrill of being used by God in spite of their flaws.

A Man Without Purpose

I like Peter, probably because I can relate to his ability to pop off without really thinking things through his words first. I admire his passion, and I envy his courage.

Mostly, I love Peter because he shows what can happen when a person is forgiven and restored. Everything changes for the better, and that gives me hope. His story is familiar, but hopefully you'll see how important it is for your own life.

Jesus' Threefold Restoration of Peter

Peter had a good heart, but he tended to bite off a little more than he could chew at times. His desire to do what's right often collided with his desire to do things in his own strength. In the last hours of Jesus' life, all of that caught up with him. He messed up in a big way (more about that later), but Jesus wasn't done with him yet. He took the first step to restore his fallen disciple. . . . which brings us to John 21:15-19.

^{15} When they had eaten breakfast, Jesus asked Simon Peter, "Simon, son of John, do you love Me more than these?"

"Yes, Lord," he said to Him, "You know that I love You."

"Feed My lambs," He told him.

^{16} A second time He asked him, "Simon, son of John, do you love Me?"

"Yes, Lord," he said to Him, "You know that I love You."

"Shepherd My sheep," He told him.

^{17} He asked him the third time, "Simon, son of John, do you love Me?"

Peter was grieved that He asked him the third time, "Do you love Me?" He said, "Lord, You know everything! You know that I love You."

"Feed My sheep," Jesus said. ^{18} "I assure you: When you were young, you would tie your belt and walk wherever you wanted. But when you grow old, you will stretch out your hands and someone else will tie you and carry you where you don't want to go." ^{19} He said this to signify by what kind of death he would glorify God. After saying this, He told him, "Follow Me!"

A Little Background

To understand the importance of this event in Peter's life, we need to back up a few pages. In John 13:36-38, Jesus had predicted His impending death. In response, Peter vowed complete loyalty—even to the point of death. That's when Jesus told Peter something he probably didn't want to hear. Rather than sticking with Jesus to the end, Peter would deny Him three times in a short amount of time.

By the time we get to John 18, Jesus had been arrested and the disciples had scattered. For his part, Peter stayed at what he thought was a fairly safe distance and watched the trial unfold from afar. Recognized as a follower of Jesus by others in the crowd, what did this MVP disciple do? He denied Jesus—not once, but three times (just as Jesus predicted he would do).

After the third denial, one gospel writer noted that Peter went away and "wept bitterly" (Luke 22:62). This is Peter on the absolutely worst day of his life. Broken, ashamed, angry at himself, confused, and scared.

The evening after His resurrection, Jesus appeared to all of the disciples except Thomas (John 20:19-24). A week later, with Thomas now present, He came to them again (John 20:24-29). So, Peter had encountered Jesus in the days following the Resurrection.

But Jesus had more to share with Peter. So, He initiated a more personal meeting with His wounded disciple.

Peter's Second Chance

Having helped the disciples haul in a major catch (John 21:1-14), Jesus sat down and ate breakfast with this group of followers—including Peter. I can only imagine the raging sea of emotions inside Peter, especially when Jesus turned and began a conversation that would change his life. Because you and I get to eavesdrop on their dialogue, we can learn some things about restoration.

1. God is in the business of restoration. Notice that Jesus didn't denounce Peter and condemn him to hell. He didn't chastise Peter in front of his fishing buddies. He didn't leave Peter as a broken man, carrying the guilt and shame of his unfaithfulness.

Instead, Jesus called him out and called Him back to Himself—and back to service. Scripture provides several instances where God promised to bring change, healing, and hope. Here are just a few:

Lord, because of these promises people live, and in all of them is the life of my spirit as well; You have restored me to health and let me live. —Isaiah 38:16

Therefore, this is what the LORD says: If you return, I will restore you; you will stand in My presence. —Jeremiah 15:19a

I will strengthen the house of Judah and deliver the house of Joseph. I will restore them because I have compassion on them, and they will be as though I had never rejected them. For I am the Yahweh their God, and I will answer them.—Zechariah 10:6

So the crowd was amazed when they saw those unable to speak talking, the deformed restored, the lame walking, and the blind seeing. And they gave glory to the God of Israel.—Matthew 15:31

Now the God of all grace, who called you to His eternal glory in Christ Jesus, will personally restore, establish, strengthen, and support you after you have suffered a little.—1 Peter 5:10

The LORD rebuilds Jerusalem;
*   He gathers Israel's exiled people.*
*   He heals the brokenhearted*
*   and binds up their wounds.—Psalm 147:2-3*

Yet I will certainly bring health and healing to it and will indeed heal them. I will let them experience the abundance of peace and truth. I will restore the fortunes of Judah and of Israel and will rebuild them as in former times. I will purify them from all the wrongs they have committed against Me, and I will forgive all the wrongs they have committed against Me, rebelling against Me.—Jeremiah 33:6-8

But for you who fear My name, the sun of righteousness will rise with healing in its wings, and you will go out and playfully jump like calves from the stall.—Malachi 4:2

These are not the words of a vengeful God who is just waiting to strike His people down when they sin. These are not the promises of a God who would toss us to the wayside because we are a bunch of misfit sinners who would never get it right. These are the words of a God who passionately loves His people and is deeply committed to bring them healing, health, hope, and honor.

You may think there's no way your life could be made whole. The things you've done wrong or the wrong things done to you may seem too large to overcome. You may feel like you can never be whole again. Don't give up on yourself. And definitely don't give up on God's love and faithfulness—or His ability to restore you. That's what He loves to do.

Think of a broken part of your life—a broken relationship, a sinful habit you can't break, a wound too deep for words. What would your life look like if that were no longer in your life?

2. Restoration takes time, but you will experience its completion.

Peter became an empowered force of God's hand, but he still had a lot to learn about being a follower of Jesus (see Acts 10 for a prime example). At the end of his life, though, Peter had become what Jesus had called him earlier—a rock. His faith was solid, even to his death. Church tradition says that this man who was too afraid to stand up against his Savior's crucifixion ended up dying the same way, willingly giving himself out of love for his Master. The restoration was complete.

God is incredibly eager to work in your life to heal and restore you, but that work takes time. Finding healing from past hurts and the consequences of past sins doesn't usually happen overnight. In the process of healing, be patient with Him and with yourself.

There is no bonus for being the first in your class to cross some finish line and declare, "I'm over it!" Just as God created each of us uniquely, the path of healing and restoration is unique to each person. God has wired us that way, so why would He set some arbitrary rule that says you have to be OK by tomorrow or else?

But the good news is this: At some point, you'll get to enjoy the fruit of your work. You'll get to look back and say, "Wow! Look how far I've come on this journey, and it's worth it now that I'm here!" Think about it this way: when a car is restored, there is an ending point somewhere. From then on, you enjoy driving it. Likewise, a house restored to a new beauty is worthless if you don't actually get to live in it.

God doesn't want you to live as a prisoner of sin. He doesn't want you to be defined by what you did or what others have done to you. There is no real joy in remaining a victim. It's a lonely, dreadful, and joy-less place. That's why God wants to heal you and restore you—so you can experience life as He intended, a life of joy and purpose and peace. He wants you to be free.

3. The healing process hurts, but the alternative hurts more. The conversation between Peter and Jesus was not a comfortable one. There was no discussion about the best fishing lures to use. Jesus just hit Peter with a tough question: *Do you truly love me more than these?*

Who or what are "these?" Many Bible scholars think that "these" refers to the other disciples: "Do you love me more than the other disciples love me?" Wow. What a question to ask Peter. Why would Jesus ask such an odd question?

Think back to an earlier moment in Peter's relationship with Jesus. Jesus prophesied that the disciples would turn away from Him on the night of His arrest by the Roman soldiers. Peter declared: "Even if everyone runs away because of You, I will never run away! . . . Even if I have to die with You . . . I will never deny You!" (Matt. 26:33,35). That "everyone" included the other disciples.

Jesus' question brought Peter back to this painful moment. In a sense, Jesus was asking, "Peter, do you remember that time when you said you'd never run away from me, even if the other disciples did? Do you remember telling me you'd be willing to die for me? Do you remember bragging about how your love for Me was greater than the love of these other men?"

Jesus asked this question (or a form of it) three times. That parallels Peter's three denials and probably cut the disciple's boastful pride to the core. It was a painful memory, but Jesus used that memory as a scalpel in the hands of the skilled Surgeon. He cut through the layers of Peter's heart because that was the most effective way to bring healing.

4. When God heals and restores you, He wants to use you. Once Peter denied Jesus, he could have gone back to being a fisherman. Some scholars think that's what he was doing in a boat the day Jesus restored him. Fishing probably could have given Peter a sense of dignity and success, but Jesus had other plans for the trajectory of Peter's life.

In John 18, Peter was the traitor, the loser, the temperamental disciple who couldn't decide where to place his loyalties. But after his restoration in John 21 and after the Holy Spirit empowered him in Acts 2, Peter became one of the most significant figures in the New Testament. Acts records that Peter preached one sermon to a crowd in Jerusalem, and 3,000 people gave their lives to Christ (Acts 2:41). Peter's example reminds us that when we receive God's restoration, He can use us in major ways.

When you have experienced the journey of healing and restoration, God can use you as an instrument to bring healing and life to others. Your healing isn't just for your own benefit. God wants you to share your story.

- The porn addict can share his story about the power of lust versus the power of the Savior.
- The anorexic can tell her story about releasing control and placing it in the hands of the One who controls the seasons.
- The verbally abused can offer hope to others, encouraging them to believe the Father of Lights instead of the Father of Lies.
- The teen girl who aborted her unborn baby can shout from the rafters that there is no sin beyond the reach of God's grace.

Like Peter, you won't be content just to go back to life "as normal." God will change the trajectory of your life, too.

What are some ways God has used you despite your past? What are some areas where you still need to find restoration in Him? What's holding you back?

Live It
How do you live out restoration?

This part of this Bible study is still unfinished—because God is still writing your story. There's no way of writing specifically about how you can live out your personal restoration because your story is as unique as your thumbprint. For now, you can think about areas of healing that have already taken place and look at how God has already used you.

In what areas of your life has God already brought healing? How are you different? How has God been able to use your story to minister to the lives of others?

Sometimes we won't see the effects of restoration this side of heaven. We won't know whom we will influence with our stories because the ripple effect keeps on going from person to person. The fact that God used you in one person's life isn't the end of your story. It's just the glorious beginning. Only when we get to heaven and see the great cloud of witnesses around us will we understand why our stories mattered, why our wounds, mistakes, healing, and restoration were significant in the grand scheme of His larger story.

But you can count on one thing: Nothing is wasted in God's economy. There are no scraps on the cutting room floor. God works it all together for your good and His glory (Rom. 8:28).

Believe me, my friend, the journey is worth the sacrifice it takes to get to the end.

Leader's Guide

NOTE TO LEADERS

You're holding a powerful tool. While *October Baby* focuses on a few specific issues, it has the potential to touch other pain points—pornography, divorce, sex, cutting, anorexia, and the like. So students in "Every Life Is Beautiful: The *October Baby* Bible Study" will be starting a journey that can bring healing, restoration, and hope.

As a small group leader, your role is significant. Approach your group in humility, vulnerability, and wisdom. And keep these things in mind:

• **Let parents know what's happening.** Family therapist Tony Rankin has noted that volunteer youth leaders (like you) don't owe students confidentiality. In fact, since parents are responsible before God for their children, maintaining secrets may actually hinder parents and keep teens from receiving the help they need. Rankin says that the best approach when asked to keep a secret is to say, "I care about you and want to make sure you can get the help you need. I will walk through this with you—but that might involve sharing what you tell me with someone else." Students also may need professional help with issues. Talk with your pastor or youth minister to locate some solid, godly, trained therapists.

• **Be sensitive to the Holy Spirit.** When your agenda and God's agenda don't coincide, adjust yourself to God's leading. If you sense the Spirit leading the discussion in a direction you hadn't planned, follow Him.

• **Be an agent of grace.** Students struggling with past sin need to be reminded that God's passionate love runs deeper than any sin or shame.

• **Stay gender specific.** Girls and guys process things differently. That's why each session includes "Girls' Perspective" and "Guys' Perspective" features. And while many of the small group activities are similar, the dynamics won't be. The topics discussed in this study require great sensitivity and freedom for students to share and process. For these reasons, we recommend that you keep your small groups separated by gender.

SESSION 1: LARGE GROUP

Before you start this first session, set the ground rules for the entire study. Explain that over the next four weeks you'll be talking about some pretty serious stuff, stuff that needs to stay within the group.

Also emphasize that each person has the right to share, so there should be no interruptions when someone is sharing. *(Encourage students not to ramble, if possible.)* Explain that if they'll really listen and trust the process, God can do some amazing things in their lives as they learn about how to deal with the worst life has to throw at them.

Open Up

Share a secret you kept as a child or a "silly" secret that you've kept for a long time (like your comic book addiction). Explain that some secrets are benign, while others are serious, painful, and damaging. Then explain that this Bible study is all about secrets: how they grow and what eventually happens when we keep dangerous secrets too long.

As an alternative, share a simple secret with a student before everyone arrives, such as the secret stash of candy or soft drinks. Watch how long it takes before this secret is shared with others. (You may be surprised by students who keep a secret—and those who don't!) From there you can springboard to the secrets introduction above.

Watch It

View Clip 1, "The Secret Revealed" (3:04) from the small-group DVD.

To set the stage, share the following summary: *In this scene, 19-year-old Hannah Lawson discovers that her parents have been keeping a secret from her—a secret about how her life began. It is a secret that will shake her understanding of who she is.* After watching the video clip, break into small groups according to gender and age.

SESSION 1: SMALL GROUPS
GIRLS' SMALL GROUP(S):

Dive In
Debrief: Allow girls to process the film clip by asking the following questions (as many as time will allow):

- **Were you surprised by the news of Hannah's biological mother?**
- **How do you think you would have responded?**
- **Why do you think Hannah's parents didn't tell her the truth?**
- **What was Hannah feeling?**
- **Have you ever felt a bit like Hannah did?**

Ask: **How do you know when a secret should be told?**

After discussion, give them the following guideline from page 8: *Fill in the blank: If you knew _____ about me, you wouldn't like/ love/accept me.* Discuss whether this is a valid rule of thumb to use when determining whether a secret should be told. Help girls understand that if a secret changes how you feel about yourself, it's probably not something to keep to themselves. *(If you knew I had an abortion; been abused; used drugs, looked at porn, etc.)*

Look at Scripture
Explain that this session will focus on one man in the Bible who created a world of trouble by trying to keep his sin a secret. Direct girls to look at 2 Samuel 11:1-15 in their books (pp. 9-10). Allow girls to read the story silently. Then dissect the story by using the summary on page 10. Use the following outline to discover the truth about secrets:

1. Secrets often stem from sinful actions.
Ask: **What sinful actions did David commit? Who was affected by David's sin?**

Direct girls to read the "Girls' Perspective" on page 12 to illustrate how secrets often stem from sinful actions. Be sure to point out that sins we commit carry their own consequences (like David). Share that other times, someone else sins, but we still feel the impact of those consequences, just like Bathsheba and Uriah.

Ask: Have you ever noticed how a secret can develop around a sin? What secrets in your own life have stemmed from sin?

Give an example in your own life, if possible. This will help girls open up.

2. Secrets pile on top of one another.
Draw a square on the bottom of a sheet of paper. **Ask: What was David's first sin? What was the next thing he did?** Draw a box on top of the first and put the answer in the box. Continue reviewing the story and drawing box upon box to illustrate how the sins piled up.

Ask: How do sins like lying pile up? Cheating? Pornography? Drinking? Walk through some scenarios that illustrate this principle. You can use the "Girls' Perspective" on page 13 to help you with this.

3. Secrets can control you.
Discuss how David became consumed with the need to hide his sin. Point out the things that he did as a result. **Ask: How do secrets control teen girls?** Allow girls to look at "Girls' Perspective" on pages 14-15 for examples. **Ask: How has a secret controlled you in some way?**

4. Secrets wear you out.
Ask: How do you think David felt when he was at the peak of his rebellion and secret-keeping?

Direct girls to read Psalm 32:3-4 in their Bibles (or on page 16). **Ask: What phrases indicate that David's secrets were weighing him down?** Challenge girls to share a time where a secret or secret sin weighed them down or wore them out. Share an example from your own life. **Ask: Why is it that we keep carrying this weight? What is your biggest fear about sharing your secrets?**

5. Secrets lose their power when shared.

Direct girls to read Psalm 32:5-6. **Ask: How do we know from these verses that secret sin no longer controlled David's life?** Discuss responses. Highlight words like "acknowledge" and "confess." Point out that David returned to a place where He trusted God, and God responded by becoming his refuge. **Ask: How do you feel when you finally share a secret that really needs to be told?**

Live It

Look at the evaluation questions on pages 17-18. Distribute pens/pencils and encourage girls to journal their responses. Explain again the power, relief, and hope that is released when secrets are shared. Allow girls to share some of their answers as they feel comfortable. *(It may take a few minutes for girls to open up. Don't be afraid of sitting in silence for a few minutes.)* Direct girls' attention to the final paragraph on page 18. Remind them that God sees all and understands all. More importantly, He loves them, right where they are.

Explain to girls that throughout the study, you'll arrive early and stay late. If they want, you will be their "safe place" for secret sharing. At the same time, remember that if a girl is being abused (or has been in the past) or is suicidal, this calls for immediate intervention and action. (Refer to your responsibility for keeping secrets and the need for professional help discussed in the "Note to Leaders" on p. 52).

Further Application: Consider creating some gender-based accountability groups in which students can talk together openly about the things they are struggling with. Meetings take place once a month. That's the place where real community happens.

GUYS' SMALL GROUP(S):

Dive In

Debrief: Allow guys to process the film clip by asking the following questions (as many as time will allow):

- **What would you do if your parents kept a huge secret from you, like that you were adopted? How would you respond to them?**
- **Why do you think Hannah's parents didn't tell her the truth?**
- **Are guys better than girls at keeping secrets? Why or why not?**
- **What's the biggest secret you ever kept when you were a kid?**

Ask: How do you know when a secret should be told? After discussion, direct them to the following guideline from page 8: *Fill in the blank: If you knew _____ about me, then you wouldn't like/love/accept me.* Discuss whether this is a valid rule for determining whether a secret should be told. Help guys understand that if a secret changes how you feel about yourself, it's probably not something to keep to yourself. *(If you knew I had been sexually active; been abused; used drugs; looked at pornography, and so forth)*

Look at Scripture

Ask guys to identify some male role models from the Bible. Write their answers on a large sheet of paper (hopefully someone will mention David). Ask why each one is a role model. Ask if any of them ever harbored a secret. Explain that one man in Scripture harbored a really big secret and suffered the consequences for it.

Direct guys to look at the Scripture on pages 9-10. Encourage them to read the story silently. Then dissect the story by using the summary on page 10. Use the following outline to discover the truths about secrets:

1. Secrets often stem from sinful actions.
Ask: What sinful actions did David commit?
Ask: Who was affected by David's sin?
Ask: Did David sin because he saw Bathsheba? Why or why not?

Explain that David liked what he saw. Share that there's no sin and no secret in that. Seeing a person as attractive isn't wrong. It's what you do about that attraction that makes all the difference.

2. Secrets pile on top of one another.

Draw a square of the bottom of a large sheet of paper. **Ask: What was David's first sin? What was the next thing he did?** Draw a box on top of the first and put their answer in the box. Continue reviewing the story and drawing box upon box to illustrate how the sins piled up.

Ask: How do sins like lying pile up? Cheating? Pornography? Drinking? Walk through some scenarios that illustrate this principle. You can use the "Guys' Perspective" on page 13 to help you with this.

3. Secrets can control you.
Discuss together how David became consumed with the need to cover up his sin. Point out the things that he did as part of his plan to keep his secret hidden. **Ask: What are some secret sins that can quickly control guys?** (pornography, bullying, steroid use, alcohol addiction, etc.)

4. Secrets wear you out.
To illustrate this point, get a backpack and some very large, very heavy stones (or other heavy objects). Call on a guy to put the backpack on. Review the sins David committed. After you mention each one, put one of the heavy stones or objects in the backpack. Continue with this process until the backpack gets really heavy. Then explain the point: **Secrets weigh you down.** Ask the guy wearing the backpack to continue standing where he is until you tell him to stop.

Ask: How do you think David felt when he was at the peak of his rebellion and secret-keeping? Direct guys to read Psalm 32:3-4 in their Bibles (or on page 15). **Ask: What phrases indicate that David's secrets were weighing him down?**

Share a time where a secret or secret sin was weighing you down or wearing you out. Allow guys to share their own stories if they're willing (but don't be surprised if they don't, especially in this first session). **Ask: Why is it that we keep carrying this weight around in our lives? What is your biggest fear in sharing your secrets? What's the downside of telling those hidden things?**

5. Secrets lose their power when shared.

Ask guys to read Psalm 32:5-7 from the Bibles or from page 16. **Ask: How do we know from these verses that secret sin no longer controlled David's life? How do you feel when you finally share a secret that really needs to be told?**

Ask the guy bearing the weight of the backpack if he'd like to drop the backpack. Make the point that instant relief came when he stopped carrying the weight on his back and shoulders. In the same way, we stop carrying the heavy weight of a secret when we finally tell it in a safe place.

Live It

Look at the evaluation questions on pages 17-18. Distribute pens/pencils and encourage guys to record their responses. Explain again the power, relief, and hope that is released when secrets are shared. Allow guys to share some of their answers if they feel comfortable. (*It may take a few minutes for guys to open up. Don't be afraid of sitting in silence for a few minutes.*) When you feel comfortable with moving on, direct guys to the final paragraph on page 18. Remind them that their secrets really aren't secrets with God. He knows and understands. More important, He loves them, right where they are.

Explain that throughout the study, you'll arrive early and stay late. If they want to make you their "safe place" for sharing secrets, this will give them opportunity to do so. Please remember that if a guy is being abused (or has been in the past), is harming someone else, or is suicidal, this calls for immediate intervention and action. (Refer to your responsibility for keeping secrets and the need for professional help discussed in the "Note to Leaders" on p. 52).

Further Application: Consider creating some gender-based accountability groups in which students can talk together openly about the things they are struggling with. Meetings may take place once a month. That's the place where real community happens.

SESSION 2: LARGE GROUP

Open Up

Prior to the lesson, print the names of several celebrities or historical figures on their own index card. *(Examples: Abraham Lincoln, Helen Keller, Justin Beiber, and so forth)* As students arrive, tape the index cards on their backs. Explain that their task is to ask yes or no questions to each other in order to discover "who they are." If you have a large enough group, add the rule that they can ask only one question to each person. Then they must mingle with others and ask another question. If you'd like, award a prize to the winner.

Watch It

View Clip 2, "I Don't Even Know Me" (4:34), from the small-group DVD.

To set the stage, share the following summary: *In this scene, the main character, Hannah, has recently learned that not only is she adopted, but also that she's the survivor of a failed abortion. Trying to process her thoughts and questions, she sits on a dock where she played as a child. Jason, her best friend (and potential romantic interest), joins her at the dock. He can sense something's wrong, and he wants to hear what's on her mind.*

After watching the video clip, break into small groups according to gender and age.

SESSION 2: SMALL GROUPS
GIRLS' SMALL GROUP(S):

Dive In

Debrief: Allow girls to process the film clip by asking the following questions (as many as time will allow):

• **Hannah says, "My whole life is a lie..." Why do you think she saw her life that way?**

- Hannah says, "I just want answers to all these questions." What questions do you think Hannah was asking?
- What questions do you think teen girls ask about themselves?
- Hannah says, "I don't even know me." When have you felt the same way? What was that like? What caused you to say that about yourself? Do you think adults ever think that about themselves?

Look at Scripture

Explain that guys and girls tend to find their significance, value, and identity in different ways. **Ask: How do you think guys find their value? Explain the information under "Guys' Perspective" on page 21. Ask: How are girls different? How do we find our value?** Explain the information under "Girls' Perspective" on page 21.

Explain that this session will focus on a man in the Bible who learned that his whole life had been a lie and how he found his real identity. Encourage girls to name all the things they can recall about the biblical character Saul/Paul. List these on a large sheet of paper. **Ask: Based on all you know about him, where do you think Saul found his identity before he became a Christ follower?**

Direct girls to read Philippians 3:3-6 on page 22. Ask them to identify how Paul measured his worth by underlining the things he valued before Christ captured his heart. Review the information on pages 22-24 to help them understand Paul's cultural context.

Explain that Paul would have said, "I am a Jew" if asked who or what he was. His Jewish heritage defined everything in his life. **Ask: If someone asked you the same question, what would you say? What things define you? Is it a talent or sport? Is it your grades? Your boyfriend? A friendship?** Allow girls to wrestle with their answers to this question.

Explain that Paul's perspective changed once he encountered Christ. Point out that Paul learned an important lesson: **Identity formed apart from Christ is flawed and erratic.**

Ask: Why is any identity formed apart from Christ flawed? Erratic?

Use the illustration of a house of cards. If time allows, group the girls into two or three teams and let each team try to build a house of cards. Make sure you "accidentally" bump the table so that no one's house gets established. Talk about the importance of building your life on something permanent. Emphasize basing your identity is Christ.

Direct girls to read Philippians 3:7-9 (from the *CEV*) on page 24. **Ask: How did Paul describe the things that he once thought were so valuable? Why? Where did Paul eventually find his acceptance?**

Explain to girls that they may have lived their lives thinking their identity was in something they did (like being a great student or being popular). They may have thought they were defined by something done to them (like being the victim of sexual or physical abuse or the target of a bully). Explain that those things are not the true source of their identity. **Say: We are all more than the sum of our mistakes. We have the choice to find our identity in something truly amazing.**

Ask: Do you think Paul was scared to leave his past identity behind him? Why? Discuss responses. **Ask: Do you think it would be scary to begin breaking away from the old standards you have used to define your value?** Talk with the girls about the emotions and fears they might feel as they redefine their identity as a beloved child of God.

Group girls into teams of two or three if possible (if you already have a small group, keep them together) and direct them to read Colossians 2:9-10 on page 26. Instruct the groups to create a billboard that would communicate the truth from the verses they just read. Provide markers and poster board to help them to make their signs.

After a few minutes, review each group's work. Allow girls to share what inspired them and how the billboards remind them of the truth of God's love and purpose for them.

Live It

Distribute pens and direct girls to fill in the blanks and answer the response questions about the potential source(s) of their identity on page 27. Quietly play music. Challenge girls to give their full attention to what God may be trying to say to them through this Bible study.

After a few minutes, share a testimony about a faulty way you once defined yourself. (You can use the bullet points/questions on p. 27 as a starting point). Allow girls to share their own faulty identities. Allow this to be a freeing time in which girls can affirm one another—not for what they do or their outside values, but because of what Christ has done for them.

Direct girls to look at the verses on page 28 that will remind them of who they are as a follower of Christ. Direct them to find the one that is most meaningful to them and to circle it. Allow time for girls to share why the verse is meaningful to them.

Challenge girls to memorize the verse(s) they circled during the coming weeks. Also direct girls' attention to the salvation prayer on page 28. Encourage them to evaluate their lives to determine if they have ever accepted Christ's offer of salvation. Let them know that you are willing to speak with any girl who needs to make that decision.

Close in prayer, asking God to work in the hearts of girls and in your own heart. Ask Him to help each member of the group to establish an identity that is solely based on God's love as expressed through Jesus.

GUYS' SMALL GROUP(S):

Dive In

Debrief: Allow guys to process the film clip by asking the following questions (as many as time will allow):

• **Hannah says, "My whole life is a lie..." Why do you think she saw her whole life that way?**

- Hannah says, "I just want answers to all these questions." What questions do you think Hannah was asking? What kinds of things do guys question?
- Hannah says, "I don't even know me." Have you ever felt the same way? What was that like? What caused you to say that about yourself? Do you think adults ever say that about themselves?
- What do you think of Jason as a person? What would you have done if you had been in his situation on the dock? What would you have been thinking?

Look at Scripture

Explain that guys and girls find their significance, value, and identity in different ways. Ask: **How do you think girls find their value?** Explain the information under "Girls' Perspective" on page 21. Ask: **How are guys different? How do we find our value?** Explain the information under "Guys' Perspective" on page 21.

To illustrate the slippery slope of identity based on works, allow guys to play a massive game of "King of the Mountain." *(Instructions: In this game, one guy stands as "king" on top of a hill or mound. Other players try to climb the "mountain" to knock the king off the hill. Once a new "king" has won the throne on top of the mountain, the game begins again.)* Create your own mountain based on the materials available. If you have a large hill nearby, you can walk to it. If you have access to lots of magazines and newspapers, stack them up and use that as the mountain. Or use pillows, couch cushions, and bean bags—anything that is slippery and unstable will work as the mountain.

After guys have exhausted themselves by trying to be king, direct guys to read Philippians 3:3-6 on page 22. Ask them to identify the things Paul used to find his worth by underlining the things he valued before Christ captured his heart. Review the information on pages 22-24 to help them understand Paul's cultural context.

Explain that Paul would have said, "I am a Jew" if asked who or what he was. His commitment to the Jewish faith defined everything in his life.

Ask: If someone asked you the same question, what would you say? What defines you? Is it your hobby? A car? Your grades? Trophies in your room? Allow guys to wrestle with their answer to this question.

Divide guys into two groups (if possible). Explain that they will take part in a debate. One side will support the following resolution: *Identity formed apart from Christ is flawed and erratic.* The other team will oppose the resolution. Give each group time to gather its thoughts and to select a spokesman. Work with teams that may be struggling with their points of debate. Allow them to debate as time allows. If you have a small group and are unable to form teams, give guys the assignment of proving the statement false while affirming the truth.

Ask: Why is any identity formed apart from Christ flawed?

Explain to guys that they may have lived their lives thinking their identity was rooted in something they did (like being a great student or the best athlete). They may have thought they were defined by something done to them (like being the victim of sexual or physical abuse or the target of a bully). Emphasize that those things are not the true source of their identity. **Say: We are all more than the sum of our mistakes. We are more than what has happened to us. We have the choice to find our identity in something amazing.**

Ask: Do you think Paul was scared to leave his past identity behind him? Why? Discuss responses. **Ask: Do you think it would be scary to begin breaking away from the old standards you have used to define your value?** Talk with the guys about the emotions or fears they might experience as they redefine their identity as a beloved child of God. **Ask: Is it too "sissy" or "weak" for guys to define themselves based on God's love? Why or why not?**

Direct guys to read Colossians 2:9-10 on page 26. **Ask: What do you consider the most significant phrase in these verses?** Discuss responses, encouraging the guys to remember they were created by God to fulfill His plans and purposes.

Live It

Distribute pens and direct guys to fill in the blanks and answer the response questions on page 27 about the source(s) of their identity. If it's not too distracting, play some music in the background. Encourage guys to take the questions seriously and to give full attention to what God may be trying to say to them through this Bible study.

After a few minutes, share a testimony of a faulty way in which you once defined yourself. (You can use the bullet points and questions on page 27 as a starting point.) Allow guys to share their own faulty identities. Help them understand that their value is not rooted in what they do, but in all that Christ has done for them.

As an option, bring in a deck of cards. Explain that trying to base your identity on anything other than the love God demonstrates for you through Jesus is like trying to build a house of cards. At any moment, it could all come tumbling down. Distribute cards from the deck along with permanent markers. Direct guys to write their faulty sources of identity (sports, abuse, addiction, past mistakes, grades, and so forth) on one side of the card as a reminder that those sources of identity are as flimsy as a house of cards.

Direct guys to read the statements and the verses about their identity in Christ on page 28. On the other side of the cards, direct guys to write down the statement/reference that is most meaningful (such as, "You have been redeemed and forgiven, Col. 1:13-14"). Encourage them to memorize the verse they have chosen. Challenge guys to keep those cards in their wallets as a reminder of where they need to be going to find their real identity.

Also direct guys' attention to the salvation prayer on page 28. Encourage them to evaluate their lives to determine if they have ever accepted Christ's offer of salvation. Let them know that you are willing to speak with any guy who needs to make that decision.

SESSION 3: LARGE GROUP

Open Up

Prior to the session, write the following sins on separate pieces of poster board: *physical/sexual abuse; terrorism; drug use; lying; gossping; murder; stealing; cheating; pornography; bullying; betrayal; cursing; abortion; adultery; alcohol use; prostitution.*

Place the cards around the room for students to see as they arrive. Explain that as a group, they must rank the sins, starting with the easiest to forgive and moving toward the most difficult to forgive. When they're done, discuss their decisions and challenge them to think critically about the actions of others and themselves. Explain that this session focuses on forgiveness. Remind students that in terms of sin, everyone is guilty and in need of redemption. Everyone is equal at the cross.

Watch It:

View Clip 3, "You Have the Power to Forgive" (6:51) from the small group DVD.

To set the stage, share the following summary: *In this scene, Hannah seeks answers in a place that was once a refuge for her adoptive mom. While in the cathedral, she meets a priest who helps her discover the power of forgiveness.* After watching the video clip, break into small groups according to gender and age.

SESSION 3: SMALL GROUPS
GIRLS' SMALL GROUP(S):

Dive In

Debrief: Allow girls to process the film clip by asking the following questions (as many as time will allow):

• **Why do you think Hannah went to the cathedral to sort out her thoughts and feelings? Why not go somewhere else?**

- **Why do you think Hannah was angry at herself? What are some of the reasons why you get angry at yourself?**
- **Do you think it's fair for Hannah to be angry at her adoptive parents? Why or why not?**
- **Of all the people in Hannah's life—her adoptive parents, her biological parents, Jason, Jason's girlfriend, herself—who do you think she would struggle with most to forgive?**
- **What was the most significant thing the priest said to Hannah?**
- **How does God's forgiveness give us the power to forgive?**

Look at Scripture

Discuss the differences between genders when it comes to forgiveness. Use "Girls' Perspective" and "Guys' Perspective" on pages 31-32 to discuss the way genders process forgiveness. Explain that this session's Scripture highlights two guys, brothers who need to reconcile.

On a large sheet of paper, create two columns and label them "Esau" and "Jacob." To remind girls of the story's background, ask them to recall facts about these twin brothers and list answers under the appropriate column. Review the back stories of the stolen birthright (Gen. 25:27-34) and the stolen blessing (Gen. 27:1-40). Explain that things got so heated at one point that Esau vowed to kill Jacob, so Jacob took off and didn't come back for more than 20 years. Only when God directed Jacob to go home did things change.

Direct girls to read Genesis 33:1-11 in their Bibles or on pages 32-33. Explain that there are several truths about forgiveness that they can discover from these verses. Briefly review these truths from pages 33-36:

- **It's never too late to forgive.**

Ask: Do you agree with this statement? Why? What happens when you hold a grudge for a long time? What's the longest you've ever stayed angry at a person? What good came of it? Point out that it had been more than 20 years, but the brothers still found a way to reconcile.

• **Forgiveness doesn't mean everything goes back to normal.**

Emphasize that forgiveness doesn't always mean that you will want to renew a relationship. Point out that the brothers went their separate ways. Remind girls that actions still carry consequences, and they will still face the consequences for what they do.

Ask: **Have you ever been in a relationship where you were wounded and didn't want to continue that relationship? Does that seem "unchristian" to not want to continue in a relationship? Why?**

• **Forgiveness is a balm that heals not only the offender, but also the victim.**

Direct girls to recall a time when they were really angry or bitter toward a person and discuss how that unforgiveness affected them. Point out that the bitterness doesn't really change the offender or the offense, but it can change the victim. Point out the effects of bitterness as listed on page 35.

Explain that there is one more key truth about forgiveness. Direct them to read Colossians 3:12-13 in their Bibles or on page 36. Group girls into teams and direct them to summarize these verses in just one sentence. After a few minutes, discuss their answers. Point out the following truth:

• **Because you have been forgiven, you have the power to forgive.**

Ask: **Why does God's forgiveness allow us to forgive others? Why can we forgive ourselves? Can you fully experience God's forgiveness and still hold a grudge? How does knowing that you are forgiven by God feel? Why are you hesitant to offer that grace and mercy to someone else?**

Encourage girls to review these four points. Distribute large note cards and markers. Direct girls to write the point that is most meaningful for them on the large note card and to decorate the note card however they would like. Instruct girls to place that note card somewhere prominent as a reminder of this truth in the coming weeks.

Live It

This portion of the Bible study session could be very powerful for girls and may surface some painful/disturbing emotions. Be prepared to help girls process what they're experiencing.

Explain that knowing a lot about forgiveness isn't enough. Share that you will be giving girls a chance to put forgiveness into action. Give each girl two pieces of paper and a pen. Instruct them to find a spot by themselves to complete the assignment. Give them the following instructions:

Sit still before God for a few minutes and ask Him to reveal people in your life you need to forgive. Write their names on one sheet of paper. When your list is complete, choose one person that you would like to forgive. Use the other sheet of paper to write a letter to that person, expressing your feelings and identifying everything he or she has done to hurt you. When you have finished this letter, say a prayer, thanking God for forgiving you. Ask Him to give you the strength to forgive that person. When you are ready, write "I FORGIVE YOU" on top of the letter. Then fold the letter.

You will want to complete this exercise beforehand and keep your letter for the upcoming activity.

As girls are working on their letters, build a small fire in a metal trash can outside. After girls return, tell them that they will have an opportunity to get rid of their letters as a symbol of their forgiveness. Take them outside and gather around the fire. If you feel comfortable, tell a bit of the story behind your letter. Put your letter in the fire and say, "I choose to forgive you because God has forgiven me." Allow girls to do the same. Explain that it's OK if they are not ready to forgive and that you can take the letter from them when they are ready.

Remind girls that while forgiveness is a choice at a point in time, it's also a process. Memories may return, giving them an opportunity to forgive again. Point out the tips for forgiveness and healing on page 39. Close in prayer. Be prepared for girls to stay afterward to talk with you.

GUYS' SMALL GROUP(S):

Dive In

Debrief: Allow guys to process the film clip by asking the following questions (as many as time will allow):

- **Hannah said she was angry at herself. Do guys get angry at themselves? Why or why not?**
- **How are girls and guys different in the ways they express anger?**
- **The priest talked about the importance of forgiveness. Is forgiving someone a "cool" or "manly" thing? Why or why not?**
- **Do you think it would be easier for a guy to forgive another person or forgive himself? Why? Do you think it's the same for girls? Why?**

Look at Scripture

To help guys connect with the struggles of Esau and Jacob, allow them to participate in an arm wrestling competition. To make things a little fairer, insist that guys wrestle with their non-dominant hand.

Prior to the lesson, put the following truths on slips of paper and hide them around the room: **It's never too late to forgive; Forgiveness doesn't mean everything goes back to normal; Forgiveness is a balm that heals not only the offender, but also the victim; Because you have been forgiven, you have the power to forgive.**

Explain that you've hidden the slips of paper around the room and challenge guys to find them. Once they've found all the pieces of paper, emphasize that these truths come from Scripture. Read Genesis 33:1-11 on pages 32-33 or in their Bibles. Review the story to make sure the guys understand what happened. Use these bullet points to explain the truths on the slips of paper:

- **It's never too late to forgive.**

Ask: Do you agree with this statement? Why? What's the longest you've ever stayed angry at a person? What good came of it? Point

71

out that it had been more than 20 years, but the brothers still found a way to reconcile.

• Forgiveness doesn't mean everything goes back to normal.

Also explain that forgiveness doesn't mean that you want to renew a relationship. Point out that the brothers went their separate ways. Note also that individuals still have to face the consequences of their choices.

Ask: Does that seem "unchristian" to not want to stay friends with someone? Why or why not?

• Forgiveness is a balm that heals not only the offender, but also the victim.

Ask guys to recall a time when they were really angry or bitter toward a person and how that unforgiveness affected them. Share that bitterness doesn't really change the offender or the offense—only the victim. Point out the effects of bitterness on page 35.

Explain to guys that there is one more key truth about forgiveness. Direct them to read Colossians 3:12-13 in their Bibles or on page 36. Ask guys to summarize the verses in one sentence. Point out the following truth:

• Because you have been forgiven, you have the power to forgive.

Ask: Why does God's forgiveness allow us to forgive others? Why can we forgive ourselves? Can you fully experience God's forgiveness and still hold a grudge? How does knowing that you are forgiven by God feel? Why are you hesitant to offer that grace and mercy to someone else?

Live It

This portion of the Bible study session could be very powerful for the guys and surface some painful/disturbing emotions. Be prepared to help guys process what they're experiencing.

Explain that knowing a lot about forgiveness isn't enough. Share that you will be giving guys a chance to put their forgiveness into action.

Prior to the lesson, create a large cross out of two pieces of wood. If making a cross is not possible, find a large tree outside near your meeting place. Also gather several hammers and several very large nails.

Distribute small note cards and pens. Direct guys to find a place by themselves to complete the following assignment:

Sit still before God and ask Him to show you one person that He wants you to forgive. Be sure to avoid rushing through this step. Once you have identified this person, write a short note to him or her, explaining how he or she has hurt you. When you have finished this note say a prayer, thanking God for forgiving you. Ask Him to give you the strength to forgive that person. When you are ready, write "I FORGIVE YOU" on top of the note card. Then fold up the note card.

You will want to complete this exercise beforehand and keep your note card for the upcoming activity.

When the guys return, tell them they'll have the opportunity to get rid of their note cards as a symbol of their forgiveness. Gather around the cross or designated tree. If you feel comfortable, tell a bit of the story behind your note card. Then nail the card to the cross or tree and say, "I choose to forgive you because God has forgiven me." Allow other guys to do the same. Explain that it's OK if they are not quite ready to forgive and that you can take the note card from them when they are ready.

Remind guys that while forgiveness is a choice at a point in time, it's also a process. Memories may return, giving them an opportunity to forgive again. Point out the tips for forgiveness and healing on page 39. Close in prayer. Be prepared for guys to stay afterward to talk with you.

SESSION 4: LARGE GROUP

Open Up

Prior to the lesson, create a computer slideshow presentation with pictures of things that have been restored. *(Examples: a classic car; a house; an old sign; a church; an antique toy; an old train; a grandfather clock, and so forth)* If you can't create a computer slideshow, just print the pictures of the items. Explain that you will be showing a series of pictures. Their goal is to discover what they all have in common. Show the pictures one by one until someone can make the connection. Award a prize.

Explain that this session will wrap up our discussion of "October Baby" and will focus on healing and restoration. Just like the "after" stories of buildings and cars, the "after" stories and pictures of healed humans are remarkable things to see.

Watch It

View Clip 4, "Thank You for Wanting Me" (3:07) from the small group DVD.

Summary:

To set the stage, share the following summary: *This clip, which takes place at the end of the movie, shows several scenes in which restoration takes place. In the end, we celebrate life—as beautifully flawed and imperfect as it is this side of heaven.*

After watching the video clip, break into small groups according to gender and age.

SESSION 4: SMALL GROUPS
GIRLS' SMALL GROUP(S):

Dive In

Debrief: Allow girls to process the film clip by asking the following questions (as many as time will allow):

- **Did you like the end of the movie? Why or why not?**
- **What people and/or relationships were healed in the final moments of the film?**
- **Which restored person/relationship was most meaningful to you? Why?**

Challenge girls to call out as many names of God as they can recall. Write them down on a large sheet of paper. Explain that they can add one name to the list, even though it is not found in Scripture: *Restorer of broken lives.* Add that name to the list you have created.

Look at Scripture

On a large sheet of paper, draw a timeline of Peter's life and direct girls to recall facts about Peter's life. As they call out the facts, also ask them to put them in chronological order on the timeline. (You'll probably have to help them.) **Ask: What were some of the most significant moments in Peter's life?**

Explain that today's session examines one of those significant moments—when Jesus restored Peter. Call on girls to read John 21:15-19 in their Bibles or on page 44. Explain the background of the passage, especially the facts surrounding Peter's claims of loyalty at the last supper and his three denials during Jesus' trial.

Ask: How do you imagine Peter felt after he denied Jesus? How do you think he felt after he found out Jesus was resurrected and alive? Why do you think Jesus asked Peter if he loved Jesus? Didn't Jesus already know? Who are "these" in verse 15?

Use the information on pages 44-49 to help girls understand that Jesus was asking some painful questions in order to heal and restore Peter.

Group girls into four teams and assign each group one of the truths from pages 45-49. Direct them to create a poster to help teach this truth to the other members of the Bible study. After several minutes, allow the teams to share their work. After all the groups have shared, **ask:**

- **Which of the Scriptures on pages 45-46 is most meaningful to you? Why?**
- **Why do you think people remain victims, even when they have the opportunity to change?**
- **Why do you think healing and restoration can be painful experiences?** (As the leader, you might want to share a personal story about a time when restoration was painful for you in order to help students see a living example.)
- **How could you imagine God using you to tell your story? What story would you tell?** (Remind girls that everyone who has been restored has a story!)

If the story of Peter's restoration was not on your timeline, add it. Ask the girls if they know what happened next in Peter's life. Talk about Peter's presence at Pentecost (in Acts 2) and the sermon he preached right after the Holy Spirit came. Call on a girl to read Acts 2:38-41. Ask girls to recall what happened. Then add this to the timeline.

Emphasize to the girls that God wants to use them—even in their broken places—for His glory. **Say: He makes broken things beautiful.**

Live It

Prior to the session, prayerfully consider what each girl in your group might be re-named to signify the work God has done in her life. Also think of some symbol that would represent that new name. For example, a girl who has been sexually abused might be renamed "Courage" because she has had the courage to face her past. You could give her a stuffed lion as a symbol.

Explain to the girls when something significant happened to a person in the Bible, God sometimes changed that person's name. *(Examples: Saul became Paul. Jacob became Israel. And Simon became Peter.)* Explain that you have given each of them a special name to signify what God has done and is continuing to do in their lives.

Begin with one girl and explain what name you've given her and the symbol representing that new name. Speak a few minutes about her and what changes you've seen in her over the last few weeks of the study. Repeat this process for each girl in your group. Allow the other girls to affirm the changes they have seen in one another.

Close this time by having girls gather in a tight circle. Explain that you would like each of them to offer a prayer, however simple, to thank God for being a Restorer and to ask Him to continue His work of healing and restoration in their lives.

GUYS' SMALL GROUP(S):

Dive In
Debrief: Allow guys to process the film clip by asking the following questions (as many as time will allow):

- **Which restoration in this movie seems most significant to you? Why? How does it reflect your life?**
- **In what ways did Jason change over the course of the movie? What can we learn from these changes in his life?**
- **Do you think Jason would be respected in your group of friends? Why or why not?**

Look at Scripture
Prior to the session, make sure you have several pieces of paper. During the session, direct guys to call out facts they know about Peter. Write each fact on a separate piece of paper and hand it to a guy. When they've named everything they can remember, direct them to stand up and to create a "human timeline" of Peter's life. If nobody recalls Peter's denial of

Jesus, write it down and give it to a guy. Do the same for the restoration of Peter. Make sure these events are put in the timeline.

Ask: On a scale of 1-10, with 1 being "mild" and 10 being "devastating," how awful was Peter's denial of Jesus?

Discuss responses, highlighting Peter's grief and remorse. Encourage guys to share about other times they have seen a guy have a complete physical and/or emotional meltdown. *(Examples: Watching someone crash on a bike; failing to get a date; blowing a big play in a game; experiencing a break-up)* If you have the opportunity, use the Internet to show video footage of some major failures.

Ask: What does it do for a guy to fail colossally? How do guys often respond when that happens? Point out that while he had definitely seen Jesus after the resurrection, Peter still needed more from Jesus. Explain that Jesus didn't allow Peter to stay humiliated and broken. He wanted healing for Peter and initiated that process one morning after Peter and some of the other disciples had gone fishing.

Group guys into four teams and assign one of the truths from pages 45-49 to each group. Direct each team to put themselves in Peter's shoes. Provide the following instructions for each team:

Read your assigned truth and its corresponding information. Write a short monologue (about five sentences) from Peter's perspective. It should explain how your truth was true of Peter's life. For example, Team 4 might write, "I know God wants to use people because He used me to…"

After several minutes, call on one person from each group to read the monologue. After groups have finished, **ask:**

- **Which truth can you relate to the most?**
- **In what ways do you think you are like Peter? In what ways do you see yourself as different from him? Why?**

- **Is there another guy that you can relate to because of the mistakes he has made? If so, who?**
- **Which of the four truths from today's session seems most important for your own life?**

Live It

Prior to the session, prayerfully consider what each guy in your group might be re-named to signify the work God has done in his life. Also think of some symbol that would represent that new name. For example, a guy who struggled with honesty might be renamed "Truth" because he has determined to eliminate lying and cheating from his life. You could give him a ruler (exact standard) with the word "truth" written on it as his symbol to keep.

Explain to guys that when something significant happened to a person in the Bible, God sometimes changed their name. *(Explain: Saul became Paul. Jacob became Israel. And Simon became Peter.)* Explain that you have decided to give each of them a special name to signify what God has done and is continuing to do in their lives.

Begin with one guy and explain what name you've given him and the symbol representing that new name. Speak a few minutes about him and what changes you've seen in him over the last few weeks of the study. Repeat this process for each guy in the group. Allow other guys to affirm what they have seen God do in each person's life, as well.

To close the session, allow guys to voice their prayers of thanks for what God has done—and continues to do—in their lives.

If you enjoyed this Bible study for students, let your church know about the adult edition.

THE OCTOBER**BABY** BIBLE STUDY

Every Life

IS BEAUTIFUL

LifeWay
Biblical Solutions for Life

This 4-week Bible study takes participants through a journey overarching themes from the m *October Baby*. Dig deep into th power of secrets, forgiveness, w you are in Christ, and restoratio through movie scenes, homewo and group discussion questions This uplifting film paired with t heart-hitting study may change the way you look at the world, y loved ones, and life.

Member Book 005506648 $6.95
Leader Kit 005508071 $19.95

To order: lifeway.com/octoberbaby | 800.458.2772
LIFEWAY CHRISTIAN STORES
Pricing and availability subject to change without notice.

LifeWay | Wom